POINT **COUNTER** POINT

MENTAL TOUCHSTONES
for the SEARCHING SPIRIT

by

K · BRADFORD BROWN

PUBLISHED 1988 BY LIFETIMES PRESS
211 BELLENDEN RD, LONDON ENGLAND
& 20 SOUTH SANTA CRUZ AVE, SUITE 303,
LOS GATOS, CALIFORNIA 95030, U.S.A.
© K. BRADFORD BROWN, 1988
PHOTOGRAPHS © JOHN COOPER, 1988
DESIGN BY DAVID TEMPLER & MAGGIE SPOONER
PRINTED BY REMOUS LTD, SHERBORNE, DORSET

AUTHOR'S PREFACE

This book is dedicated to the Searching Spirit, and is the second in a series of three volumes. The poems are themselves arranged in a sequence which expresses the progress of my own inner journey: a personal experience of the work of becoming a warrior of the spirit. This is not the story of a disciple, or a guru. It reflects the early stages on a path of inner development.

It comes with an invitation to step onto that path, and explore its meanings as they relate to the meanings of your own life.

All the thoughts expressed in this book are my own, yet the ideas of many people are inherent in each sentence. I acknowledge my teachers, family, and the many friends who will recognise their contribution to the spirit of these pages.

A very special acknowledgement is due to David Templer and Maggie Spooner for the energy and vision which has brought these books to publication.

T O U C H
S T O N E S

INTRODUCTION

Mental touchstones for an inner journey

The touchstone was once an instrument of alchemy, an assayer's device used to test the purity of gold.

Today the word still carries the meaning of a measure, a test of true authenticity, like a 'yardstick' or 'rule of thumb': a point of reference that puts us in touch with some basic, underlying constants.

Each of the poems in this trilogy is intended to serve as a kind of touchstone, a point of contact with a basic, underlying truth by which the truth of our emotional and spiritual lives may be measured.

They are short, aphoristic, and yet they are not quite 'aphorisms': aphorisms offer a comforting banality, they please us because they confirm what we always thought we knew.

These poems evoke another kind of knowing. Like the classic Zen koān they have a disquieting, paradoxical quality which presents a challenge to our 'rationality', in a form that our rationality cannot ignore. They ring of the truth but they remind us that there is something contradictory about the truth itself, which confronts our easy, everyday acceptance of the obvious.

They are meant to be used. When you are feeling lost, they will bring you back to earth. At times when you are struggling, they will make things seem simple. And when you are feeling hopeless, they will make you laugh.

As Ivor Cutler wrote:

> *"Please mister,*
> > *will you be my touchstone?*
> *Sitting by you*
> > *sets me straight . . ."*

DT

I am indebted to
the following mentors

Men go out to gape at mountain peaks,
at the boundless tides of the sea,
the encircling ocean and
the motions of the stars,
and yet they leave themseleves unnoticed;
they do not marvel in themselves.
St Augustine

The greatest derangement of the mind
is to believe in something
because we wish it to be so.
Louis Pasteur, 1876

C O N T E N T S

JOURNEY

Don't wait
to be ready.

Everything you
need for this
journey
is available
to you
right now.

Life's first commandment:
        Wake up.
Life's intermediate commandments:
        Wake up.
Life's last commandment:
        Stay awake!

How is it
that some people
can live
a lifetime
and never
ask
who am I?

I t all ends
      and begins
          with death
               and resurrection
      exemplified
          in a thousand
               different forms
          and faces.

Never didn't.

Life is
the greatest
stimulant
you
will
ever
need!

We have inadequate language
to describe our
experience
of "it",
because "it"
is not yet
our
experience.

If you get it
    it will be
        in spite of
            any method
                you use.

That's how
    it works.

And you
    need a method.

When all else fails
    don't pray to God
        to fix it.
He's not the local repairman,
    but the gremlin
        in the
            works.

God
comes to us
in many disguises.

Are you noticing
which one
He is wearing
now?

"The Kingdom of Heaven
is at hand" means
there is another order
or dominion
present
that we are not
noticing.

That we do not notice
does not excuse us
from the consequences
of acting
or believing that
no such thing exists.

Our lives are based
on compromises.

In this domain
it is either or.

We are doing it
or we are not.

And there are
no deals.

It's easier
    when you
        trust the process
    whether
        you are being
nailed to a cross
        or
    having your teeth pulled.

God
does not require us
to be
what we
ought to be,

but
what he
has already
made us,

and
that
is enough.

Before you start
　　any journey
complete the last one,
or you'll discover
　　the old and new path
　　　are on
　　　　an inevitable
　　　　collision
　　　　　course.

Love
is
the
only
way
in
and
the
only
way
out.

GIVENS

We have
no true
control
over the
outcome
of anything
important
to us.

People are
    where they are
        for the best
           of all reasons:
    they learned it.

That's the
        bad news,

     and the
        good news.

We're
all
in a
box
and
the instructions
for
getting
out
are
on the
outside.

Each new moment
　　is an opportunity
　　　　to begin,
　　　　　　because we are
　　　　　　　　always beginning
　　　　　　　　anyhow.

Blasphemy
　　is our unwillingness
　　　　to make the start,
　　　　　　while we settle
　　　　　　　　for all the good
　　　　　　　　reasons
　　　　　　　　we didn't
　　　　　　　　　or won't.

Godis that
which we
experience
when
we encounter
life
exactly
as - it - is.

For every
    inner awakening
       and growth step
   some
     sacrifice,
       some
         little death
      is required.

At times
life is packaged
as suffering.

You can
escape it . . .
by dying.

Living for the truth,
　　by the truth,
　　　　under the truth,
　　　　　　and within the truth
is guaranteed
　　to awaken you
　　　　and keep you awake.

It is also
　　guaranteed to
　　　　lose you
　　　　　　a lot of friends,
　　until you
　　　　make some more
　　　　　　for whom
　　　　　　　　truth lives,
　　　　like you.

Most
love
isn't.

What we like
we call
good.

What we don't
we call
bad.

Then we become
little Gods,
but with
clay feet
and
dirty bottoms.

My need
of
you
is not
my love
for you.

All negative emotions
are results
of lies
we
tell ourselves
and
are not noticing.

The
   Prince
            of
               lies
   does
      not
         appear
   to
      rule
         the world.
Have
   a
      closer
         look.

In spite
　　of what
　　　　your mind
　　　　　　may think,
　　the holy
　　　　of holies
　　　　　　does not lie
　　　　　　　　between your
　　　　　　　　　　ears.

A largely
　　unbridled
　　　　undisciplined
　　　　　　mind
　　　　　　　　does.

Religion is man's
invention.

God is God's
invention.

An intention
   is a way of
      holding things
         in my
            mind,
      a way of
         creating space
            for things
               to happen.

Expectations
   create a claim
      on what
         will happen
      and unnecessarily
         prejudice
            the outcome.

I
  have
    become
        my
          true
            intentions,
  and
    there
        is
        no
          excuse
  I
    can
      appeal
        to.

It is difficult
    to understand God
because
    He acts
        so much
            like
                Himself.

OPPORTUNITIES

I am constantly
    defining myself
        anew
    in every life situation

How do I
    understand
        who or what
            I am
        now and now
            and now
            and . . .

The choice
is succumbing
to your
fate,

or fulfilling
your
destiny.

No choice
is
a
choice.

What is the
    greatest pain?
To lose myself
    and fall back
    into self justification
        and
            blaming.

I can't miss
    because the target
        is directly
            in front of me.

If I don't
    take aim
        I become
            the target.

It is
    very important
        to stop
            demanding.
It is
    more important
        to notice
            I am.

If you haven't experienced
  despondency
      despair
          and
              fear
          on the Path,
  you probably
      missed it
          a little ways
              back,
  and it's
      just ahead.

Many of us
will begin
this work
by simply
learning
to wipe
our
own
behinds.

Getting agreement from others
about your condition
is a narcotic
you don't need.

Sharing the state
of your soul
you cannot
do without.

If we would
talk less
about it,
we would
speak more
of it.

True enlightenment
    begins with unloading
the truckloads of garbage
    we've been saving,
thinking we could market it
    some day.

We
   attract
      to ourselves
         exactly
            what
       we fear
          most,
until
    we dispel
       the
         fear.

The greatest gift
God can give
to us
is the
mirror.

"**M**irror, mirror on
the wall
who is fairest
of them all?"

Silly lady
when will you notice?

It's not Snow White.

Believing in God
    is a warm bath
        you don't need.

Opening your heart
    to your enemy
        is a little death
            you can't
                do without,
        if you are
            to know the God
            you are
                believing in.

Love
doesn't
cast
out
fear.

Truth
dematerialises
it.

All significant
communication
begins
and
ends
with
telling
the
truth.

Opportunities

fate	destiny
fearful	at one
knowing	un-knowing
external	internal
changing it	living it
future	present
then	now
resentful	forgiving
pleasure	serenity
self indulging	disciplined
no	yes
yes	no
things	no-thing
controlling	letting be
selective	indiscriminate
love me	love you
tight-fisted	open-handed
hope	faith
suspicious	thoughtful
closed-minded	open-minded
withdrawn	expansive
defensive	exploring
lying	truth-telling
demanding	offering
credit	satisfaction

Finding
  Him
      is
        not
          seeing
            Him.
Seeing
  Him
      is
        not
          knowing
            Him,
But
  loving
      Him
          is
            to
              know
                Him
          see Him
              and
                find Him.

QUESTIONS

"**B**rother sun
sister moon."

What
did
Francis
know
that
we
don't?

You are always
in a relationship with God
because everything
is God
was God
will be God.

Your concern
is the quality
of that relationship.

If we
　　are looking
　　　　at red
　　we can't
　　　　see blue.

How many
　　other things
　　　　can't we see
　　　　　　because of
　　what we
　　　　are seeing?

Contemporary wisdom
   reminds us
      that heaven is
         not "up there"
         or "out there".

So, why don't
   we act
      like it?

It is questionable
	that anyone knows
		what being
			truly spiritual is.

It is a dictionary
	for each new generation
		to make
			in the light
		of contemporary
			history.

Mother said,
   If you fell in a
      crap pile you'd
         come out
            smelling good.

I certainly
   went to great lengths
      to prove her
         wrong.

Didn't we all?

It looks
    like we
        took
           a fall,
   did we?

Most positive thinkers
have not flushed
their toilets . . .

forgot they
have plumbing
like the rest
of us.

Have they
lost their
sense of smell
as well?

If no one knows
    what is truly right and wrong,
      good or bad,
   if it is true
      that it is we
         who are free to decide,
  don't we want
      the rule book back,
        and the chains?

Why do we bless
the food we eat
which was blessed
in its creation?
Thanks would help . . .
not the Creator
but the receiver.

When
was
the
last
time
you
rocked
your
baby?

Who or what is
crumbling your cookie
is an important
observation.

Have you noticed
what is on your
hands
lately?

You love me when
I do
what you
like.

And when I don't?

Spirituality is a joke
        God plays on us
    to see
        if we
            will
                get
                    it.

Have you noticed?
Life
   is
      perfectly
         imperfect.

When the inevitable
 onslaughts come,
    do not ask
        what shall I do
    but rather,
        what shall I be.

If prayer or
meditation is what
the spiritual way
is all about
why didn't Jesus
give seminars on prayer
rather than
getting hung on a cross?

Everything
is a
metaphor.

Question is:
what is
the
metaphor
for?

Asking
the right question
is the doorway
to the
right answer.

CHOICES

Sometimes we
can't see the
way out
or the way through,
because
this is
the way.

All that is needed
is one more step,
and then another
and another . . .

Every moment,
   every event,
      without exception
         is a test of our
            willingness
         to discover
            new willingness
         to discover the
            new possibility
               and act
            upon it.
Always there is an implicit question:
   Are you willing?
      Now are you willing?
         And now?
            And now?
               And now?
The question is implicit even
   as we draw our last breath.
      Are you willing?
         Even now?

Some of your choices
will create
powerful
consequences
which last a long time.

Rejoice that a debt
is being paid,
and
go on.

When
you conclude
you have
no options
you can be sure
you just
lost
a
battle.

Dead end:

"Don't confuse me with
    the facts
my theories
    about the Path
        are
            made
                up."

While I shall always
   seek
      my own good,
   I can never
      be sure
         what it is.

The desire
    for happiness
        will get you
            to the
            starting line,
but not
        to the
            finish.

The warrior may set off on
     his journey
          willingly.
If he has no clear destination
     his willingness
          will lead him haplessly
               into the first snare.

True change
comes through
taking
radical
responsibility,
not
through
hoping.

Trying
didn't get us to the moon
or distant stars,
nor, did it get us
out of bed this
morning.
Worse,
neither will it let us
sleep in.

The point is:

you haven't
            done it
                    until
                        you've
                            done it.
And
    that's
        it.

Remorse
　is the mind's
　　devious invention
　to fool us into
　　believing that
　　　we have turned
　　　　from our missdeeds.
Scratch remorse
　and its partner,
　　anger
　　　will bite
　　　　your finger off.

Righteous indignation
seldom is.

Look for it
as a cloak
for self-righteous
revenge.

The real change
     cannot be the ego
          working on itself.
It requires
     the Truth revealing
          the Truth
               to the Truth
                    within oneself.
There is the
     further requirement
          to say yes.

A spiritual warrior
without a dream
is like a knight
without armour.
Any dream will do
for a while,
but a highly polished one
works best.

Don't say
   you
      don't
         believe
            in
               God.
You
   live
      and
         die
            for
               one
   every
      day.

Beware the teacher
who preaches peace
and
advocates
killing
to achieve
it.

An intention
is a vision
of something
we want
to manifest.

It will be
corrected
modified
and transmuted
to give us
exactly
what
we
get.

The masterful intention
is to want
exactly
what
we
get.

If you
    compare
        your
           internal
              movement
      with others,
you
    won't
      have
        theirs,
          or
            yours.

Life is
   evoking us
      to witness
   to what
      we know
        see
        and
        feel.

If we
   do not
      it is very likely
        fear
   has won
      again.

You can't be sure
   you are making
        the right choices,
   but
       no choice
           sure isn't
               the right one.

Faith
  is another way
    of saying
      you'll get up
        in the morning
      and go for it.

Faith in God
  is a way
    of saying
      it's not for
        no reason.

The critical reality
worth knowing:

This
is
it.

The critical question
worth asking:

Will
I
choose
it?

Love
is
not
a
feeling
but
a
choice
of
gracious
will.

BREAKTHROUGHS

Love
offers
no
resistance,
therefore
it
misses
nothing.

The connection
  between
    the heart
      and mind
    is clear.

One enlightens
    the other . . .
        slowly.

The love
   and enlightenment
      you rejoice about
         in others
      is the awakening
         of the
            same thing
               in you.

How else
   would you
      have recognised it?

When
power
is
love,
love
is
power.

When I
cease resenting,
I end part
of the
Cold War
between
America
and
Russia.

Loving
is
the
heart's
greatest
sacrifice.

Jesus . . .
Jesus . . .
Jesus . . .

Warrior's warrior.

If you learn
    to die to yourself
        regularly
    and discover
        the meaning
            of resurrection,
    physical death
        will be
            just another one.

I didn't know
what it was
to live
until I died
the first time
to my conviction
that I knew
how things ought to be.

Since then
the work
has been
to remember.

Our humanity
and our
divinity
are married,

when we are
ourselves.

Nothing
this good
can be
this simple.

Tell
it
to a sunset.

I don't know about
past lives
but from what I know
about this one,
I want
to make it count.

Spiritual work begins
    with what you are
        and what you have
            with no regrets.

The next step
    is to celebrate.

Contrary to popular
opinion,
breakthroughs
do not
have
to be
ruptures.

The
real win
is
when
people win
with
me.

Each of us
    walks upon
        his own path
            each passing hour.

Does a fish
    in the ocean
        seek the sea?

Or the bird
    find its flight?

It is only to awaken
    in the next moment
        with eyes to see
    "the path
        hath found thee".

The
  hardest
      part
        is
            believing
  that
      it's
          all
            as
                simple
  as
    trusting
        how
            it
              is.

You
don't
have
to
believe
in
God
to
believe
in
God
no matter what
"they"
say.

GIFTS

Since you
        can't buy
            love,
    how about receiving
            it as a
                    gift?

Only your
        pride
            will hurt.

You will
        come forth,
as if
        from the grave,
when
        your vision
                is great
                        enough
                    to awaken you.

Because God
　is present
　　in everything
　　　in every moment
　there is
　　no eternal God
　　　to attain,
　only a
　　yes
　　　to right now.

The life
you really
want
is a
choice,

and it takes
exactly
one second
to have
it.

Bind me
　　imprison me
　　　　shut me up.

I am
　　still as free
　　　　as I choose
　　　　　　to be.

Νο one
knows
what you
should do
or
should have done,
not
even
you.

The ego
is the freedom
of the mind
to select
an alternative
to God.

Face it.
If waking up
is the prize,
wouldn't life
give you
everything
that is going on
in your
life
right now
to accomplish it?

What's next
is
what's next.

Your mental devils
were once
the best
resources
of your
mind.

When the sacred
is secular
and
the secular
is sacred,
we will see
another
change.

God's dominion
　　is sovereign
　　　　over all other
　　　　　domains
　　　　　　　of existence.

The conditions and "rules"
　　of this dominion
　　　　transcend,
　　　　　　supercede,
　　　　　　　and
　　　　transform
　　　　all
　　　　　others
　　　　　　　in its path.

In this
domain
the darkness
and the
light
are
not
different.

The Spirit of God
   is upon
      you . . .
         never wasn't.

You
didn't
go
through
all
this
for
nothing.

When we are clear
    we deliver ourselves
        from imagination,
        illusion
                and
                    lies.

Objectivity is at hand.

Only then
    may we be
        truly free
            to create
    our lives
        and our
    world.

There are no
   extraordinary
      people

   only ordinary people
      who do
         extraordinary
            things
      with what
         they have
            been given.

If the only prayer you say in your life is "thank you", that would suffice.
Meister Eckhardt

DR. K. BRADFORD BROWN
Psychotherapist, Episcopal clergyman,
teacher, and with W. Roy Whitten, M.Div.,
co-founder of The Life Training Programme.